vanilla manila folder games
for young children

jane a. caballero, ph.d.

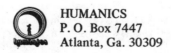

HUMANICS
P. O. Box 7447
Atlanta, Ga. 30309

HUMANICS LIMITED
P. O. Box 7447
Atlanta, Georgia 30309

PRINTED IN THE UNITED STATES OF AMERICA
ISBN 0-89334-059-6

acknowledgements

My thanks go to C. T. Caballero for his photographic
work presented in this text and to Mary Beguiristain
for her artistic assistance.

My thanks also go to my students at the University of
Miami and Morris Brown College, Atlanta University
Center who encouraged me to use these folder games
for teacher training. I would like to thank the faculty
at the University of Miami, especially Drs. Alma David
and Mark Murfin who gave me the initial opportunity
to develop these games.

CONTENTS

pre-reading

mathematics

general readiness

introduction
vanilla manila
folder games
for young children

A simple file folder, these patterns, and colored marking pens are all you need to make your own VANILLA MANILA FOLDER GAMES. You can make variations as suggested or use your own imagination to individualize folders based on the child's developmental level.

These unique folders encourage the educator to take an active role in designing the curriculum for the child. It is not a ready made kit that merely requires presentation.

Children can readily identify with the folders and are enthused when they see their teacher actually making the folders for them. They are also motivated when allowed to make their own folders.

These practical folders not only are inexpensive to develop, but also are easy to store. The curriculum folders meet the educational objectives in the early childhood period of development, approximately 3-8 years of age.

They require only a minimum amount of adult instruction. Therefore, they are ideal for parent use as well. Areas of the curriculum that are covered are: general readiness, pre-reading and math.

Opportunities for using the folder games are endless. Parents, classroom teachers, and paraprofessionals, all can adapt and use them as teaching aides to help eliminate boredom and stimulate the child's learning process.

So let's begin...

Since you will want to individualize your folders, lettering has been omitted. The following alphabet chart will assist you in lettering your folders.

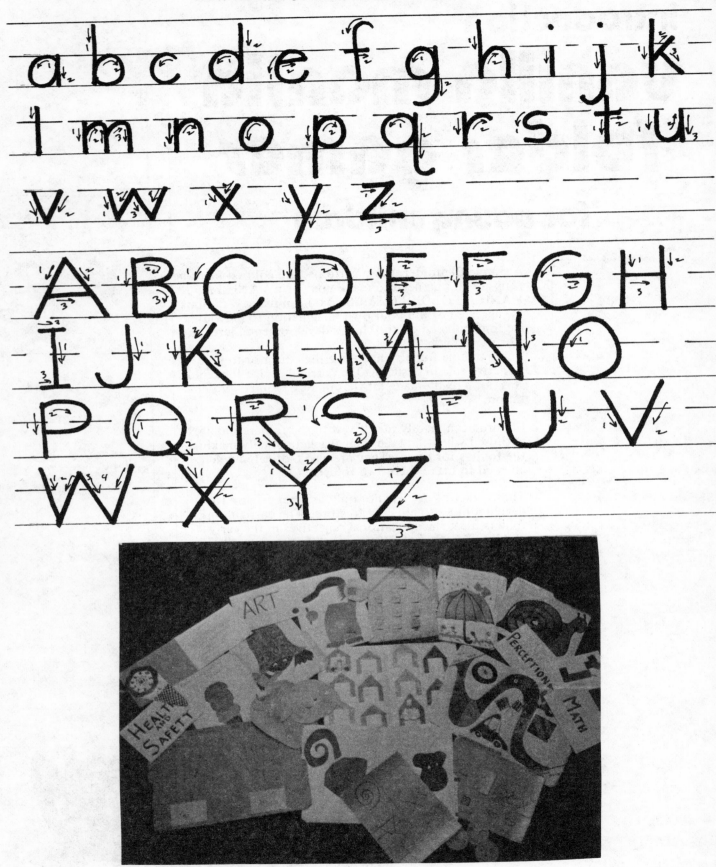

The covers are colorful pictures to attract the child's attention. You may use any picture, card, or drawing you wish on the cover. Just be sure they are bright and attractive.

part I
pre-reading

Name: Word House

Skill: Antonyms

Procedure: The child (or adult) says the word on the window.
The antonym of that work is stated. The window
is opened and the correct word appears.

Variations: Substitutions for the antonyms may include math
facts - answers, pictures - initial letters, numeral - number
word, word - vowel or blend underlined or syllable division.

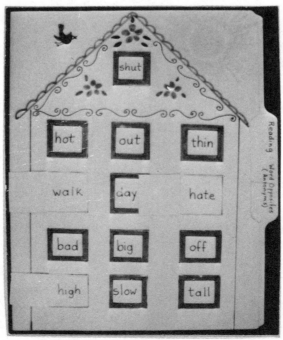

Cut 3 sides of window and write your words on the outside and inside of the window.

WORD HOUSE

8

Name: Let's Play Ball

Skill: Word Families

Procedure: The strip is slowly pulled through the ball allowing various words to be formed.

Variations: Various math combinations that total the same sum (or difference) may be substituted.

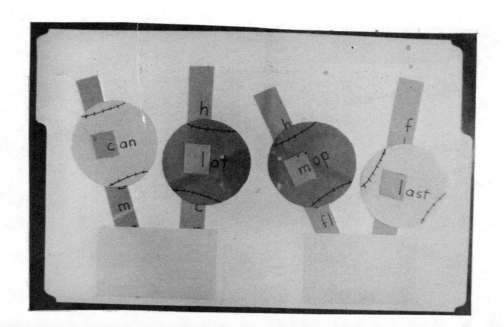

LET'S PLAY BALL

10

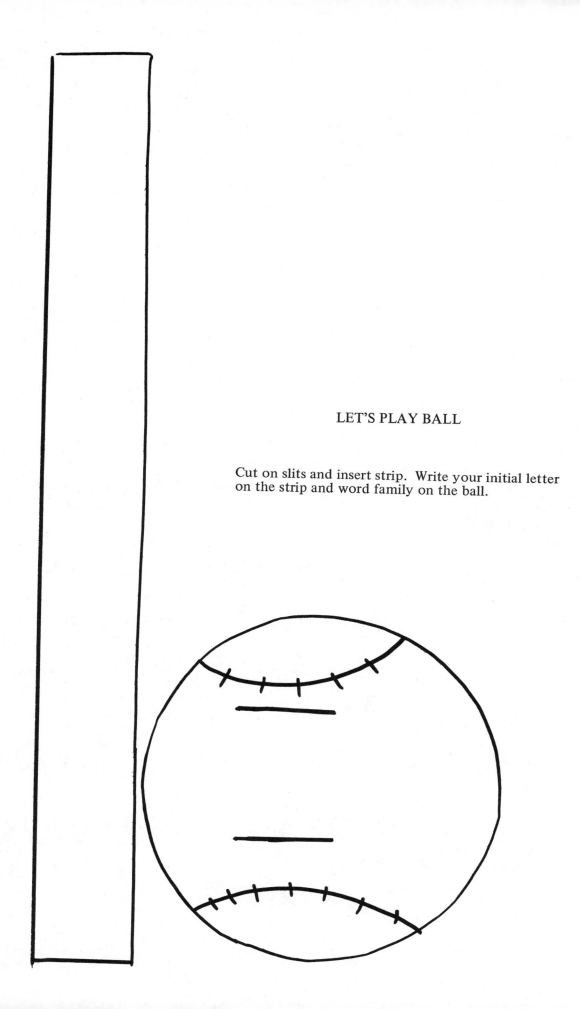

LET'S PLAY BALL

Cut on slits and insert strip. Write your initial letter
on the strip and word family on the ball.

Name: Toss the Coin

Skill: Word Recognition

Procedure: The child may play be himself or in groups. The coin
is tossed and the child must answer correctly the word
that the coin lands on to receive a point. (Fine muscle
coordination is also developed.) The key under the flap
allows for self correction.

Variations: Any vocabulary word, math combination may be used.
The child may also be asked to divide the word, find the
vowel, etc. The game may be transferred to a large poster
board and placed on the floor.

purple	red	brown
orange	blue	gray
white	green	pink
black	yellow	violet

Name: Assignment Cards

Skill: Reading and Following Directions

Procedure: The child reads the directions and completes the self directed assignments.

Variations: Any self directed assignments may be listed.

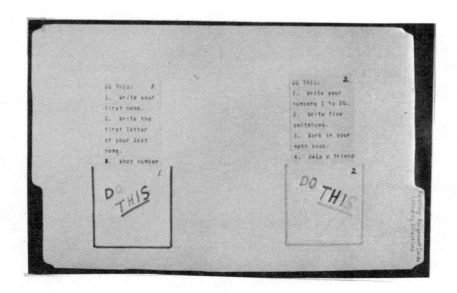

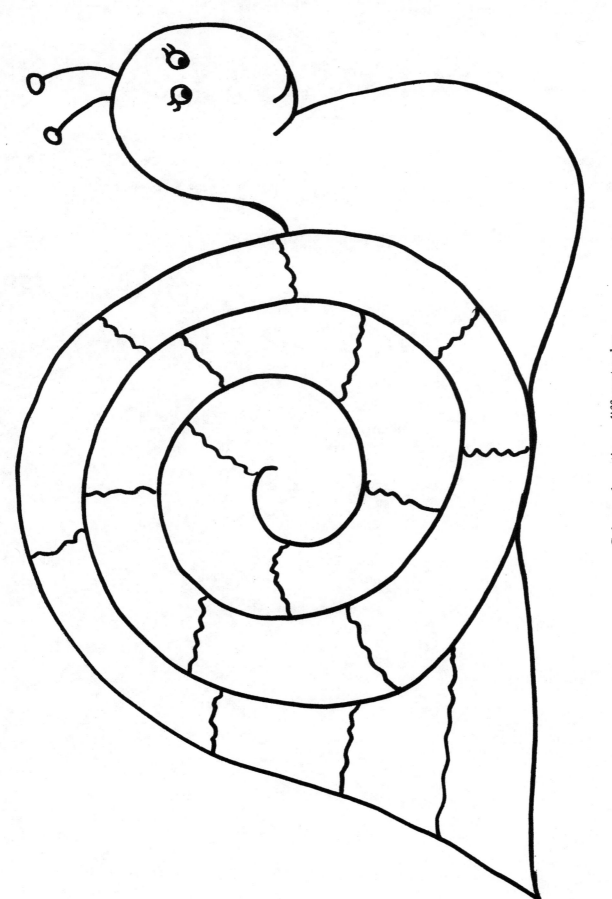

Color each section a different color.

Do this:

1. Write your name.
2. Write the numbers.
   1 to 10.
3. Draw a circle.
4. Draw a square.
5. Write a word.
6. Write a sentence.
7. Draw a triangle.

Do this:

1. Make my bed.
2. Clean my room.
3. Dust the furniture.
4. Do my homework.
5. Be very quiet.
6. Take out the trash.
7. Read a book.
8. Help Mommy.

Name: Find the Sequence

Skill: Arranging Pictures in Sequence

Procedure: The child is familiar with a given nursery rhyme. He arranges the pictures representing that story in sequential order.

Variations: Provide more detailed stories and more pictures to arrange.

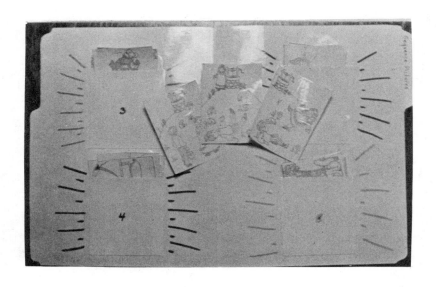

FIND THE SEQUENCE

Cut out or draw sequence pictures. (Comic strips also provide good examples.)

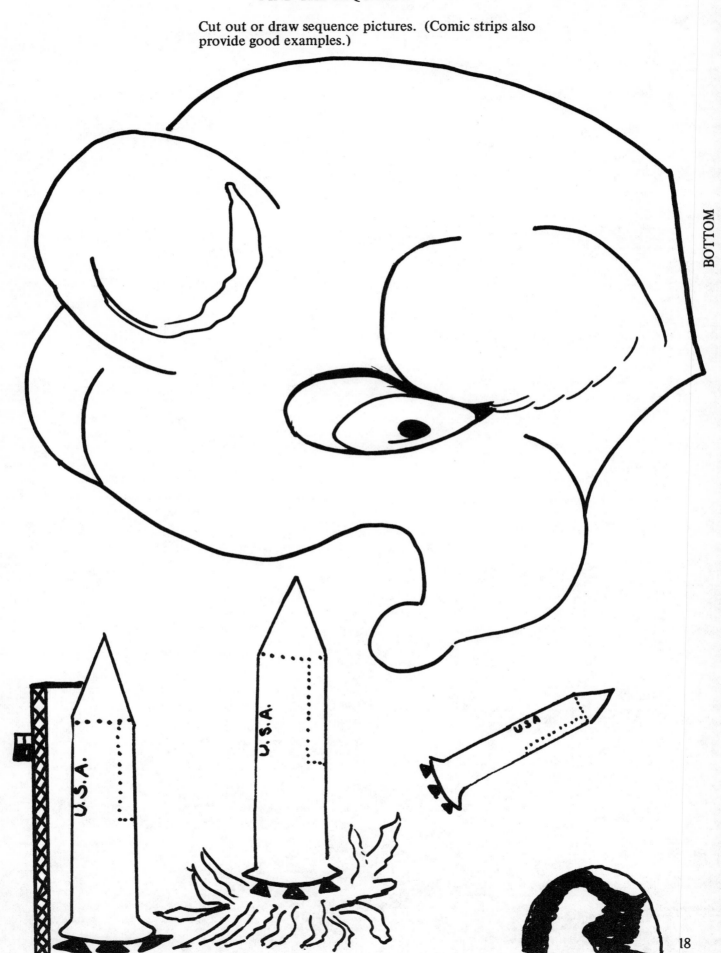

BOTTOM

18

Name: Opposites-String Match

Skills: Antonyms

Procedure: The child reads a word then locates its opposite. The string is wrapped around the brad. Figure ground discrimination is reinforced as the child locates and crosses the strings.

Variations: Any antonyms, homonyms or math combinations can be substituted.

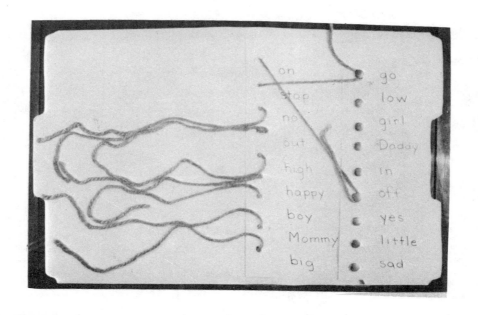

MATCH THE OPPOSITES

Name: Color Words

Skill: Recognition of Color Words

Procedure: The child places the color word card under the color
square. He then lifts the answer card to see the correct
response.

Variations: Any self correcting activity may be substituted such as
math combinations, sets and numbers, numerals and number words.

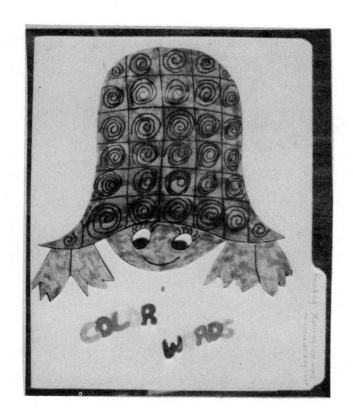

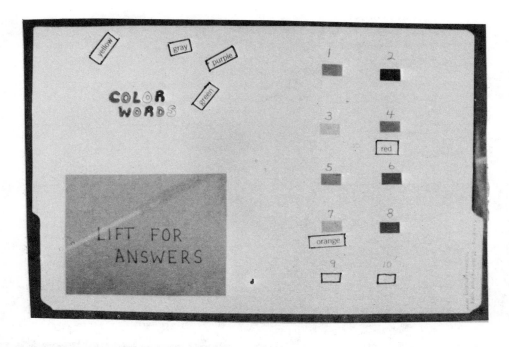

Name: Sequence Train

Skill: Placing Words in Sequential Order

Procedure: The engine contains the initial word and the following cars are
to be placed in sequential order. The correct number is on the
back of the cars.

Variations: Other sequential concepts may be noted on the train (months, days,
number words.

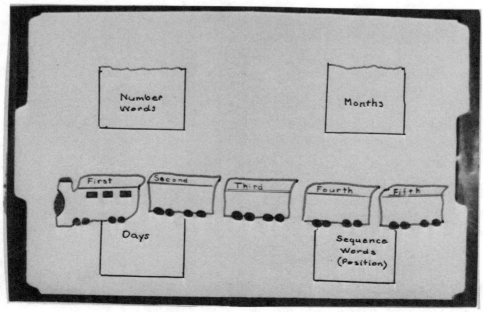

TRAIN SEQUENCE

24

Write your sequence words on the trains.

25

Name: Alphabet Puzzle

Skill: Puzzles of the letters reinforce letter shape and recognition.

Procedure: The puzzle pieces are arranged on top of the letter noted.

Variations: All letters and numerals may be used.

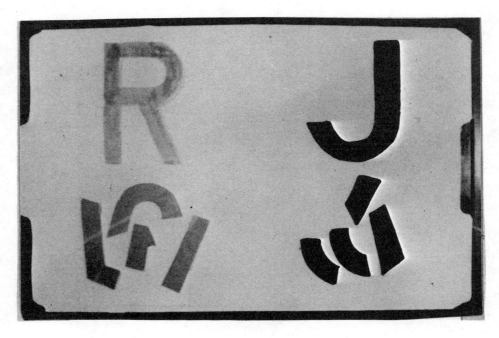

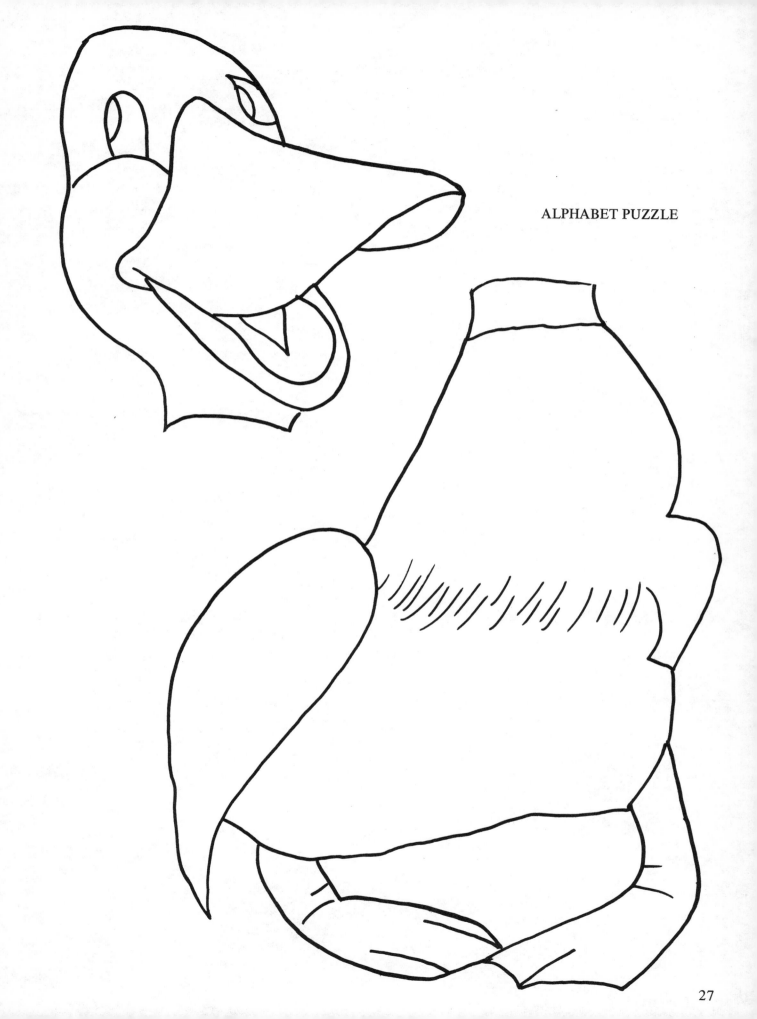

ALPHABET PUZZLE

27

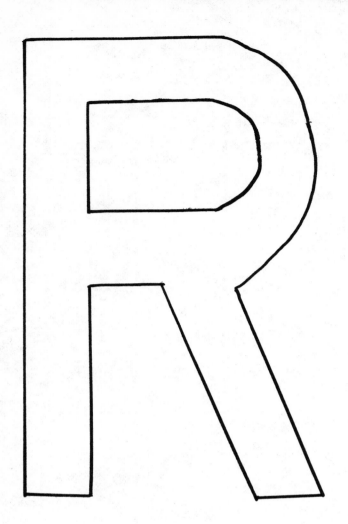

ALPHABET PUZZLE

Cut 2 of each letter. Cut 1 letter into pieces. All the letters of the alphabet can be made.

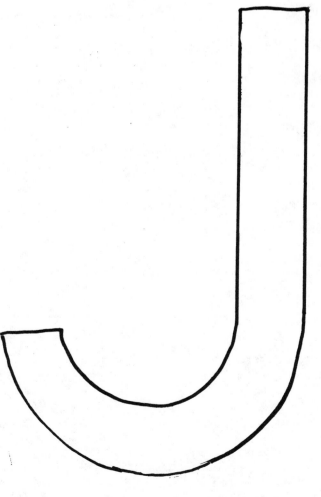

Name: Alphabet Match-Upper and Lower Case Letters

Skill: Awareness of and matching upper and lower case letters.

Procedure: The child matches the card with the upper case letter to the card with the lower case letter. The cards may be color coded for the initial step , then they may be changed to all one color.

Variations: Words can be written on the card and the card may be cut in half. The child will match the two pieces.

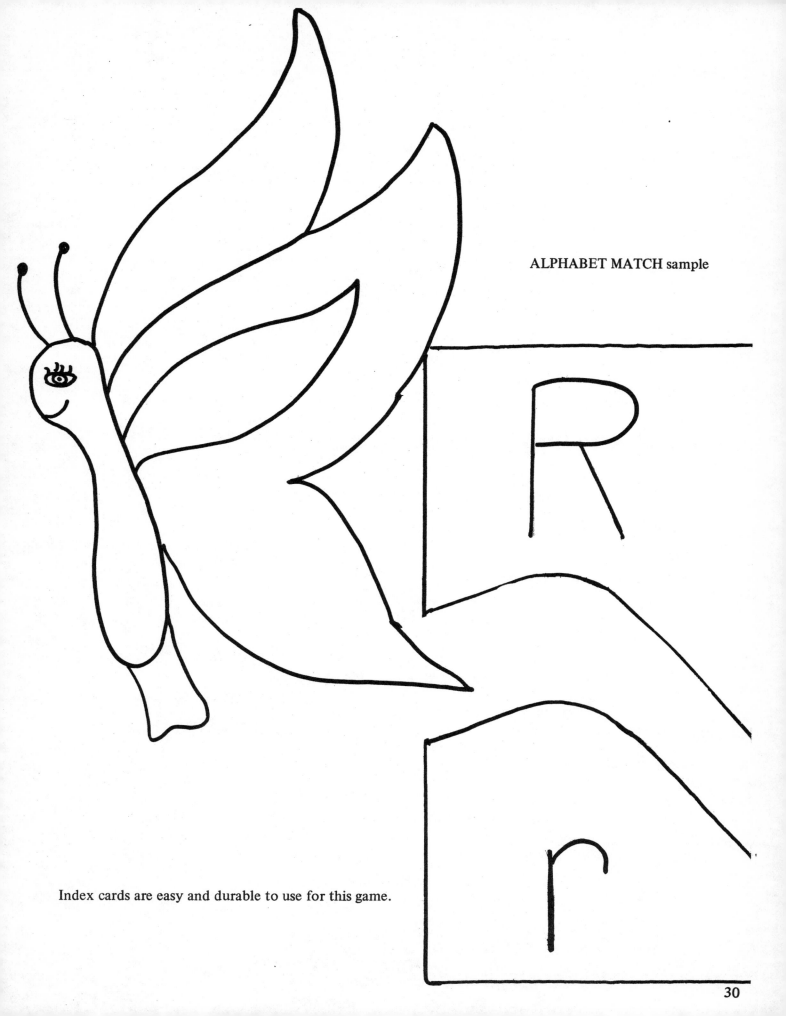

ALPHABET MATCH sample

Index cards are easy and durable to use for this game.

Name: The Great Race

Skills: Letter Recognition and Reinforcement.

Procedure: One or more children may play. A die is thrown and the player moves his race car the number on the die. He must say the letter on the square if he is to remain. The procedure is continued until there is a winner. Additional objectives include one-to-one counting and social interaction.

Variations: Any symbol may be substituted for the letters: numbers, math combinations, vocabulary words.

GREAT RACE

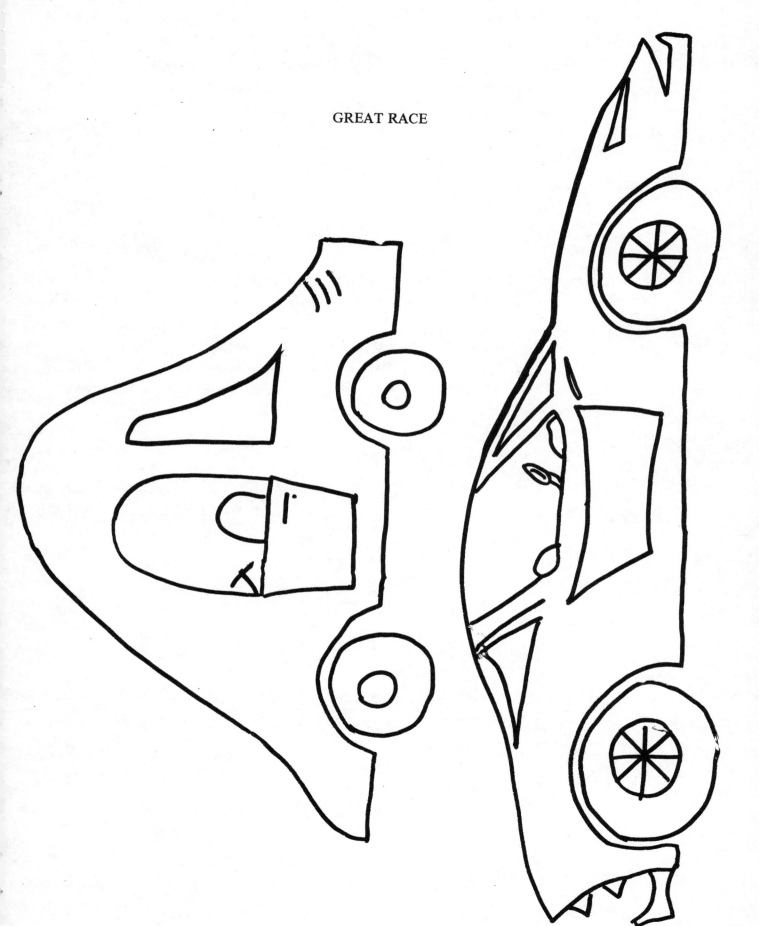

Name: Brighten Up Your Visual Discrimination

Skill: Visual Discrimination-Letter Combinations

Procedure: The child places the card in its corresponding envelope. Note:
Red lines at the bottom of the card and envelope to help the
child place the card the right direction.

Variations: The letter combinations may be substituted for symbols, words,
and single letters.

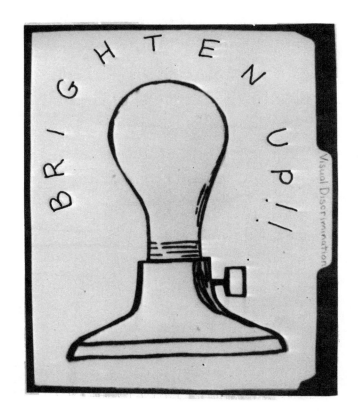

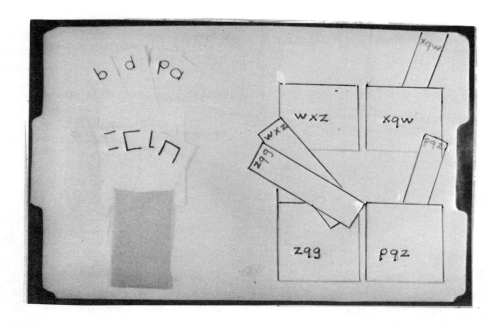

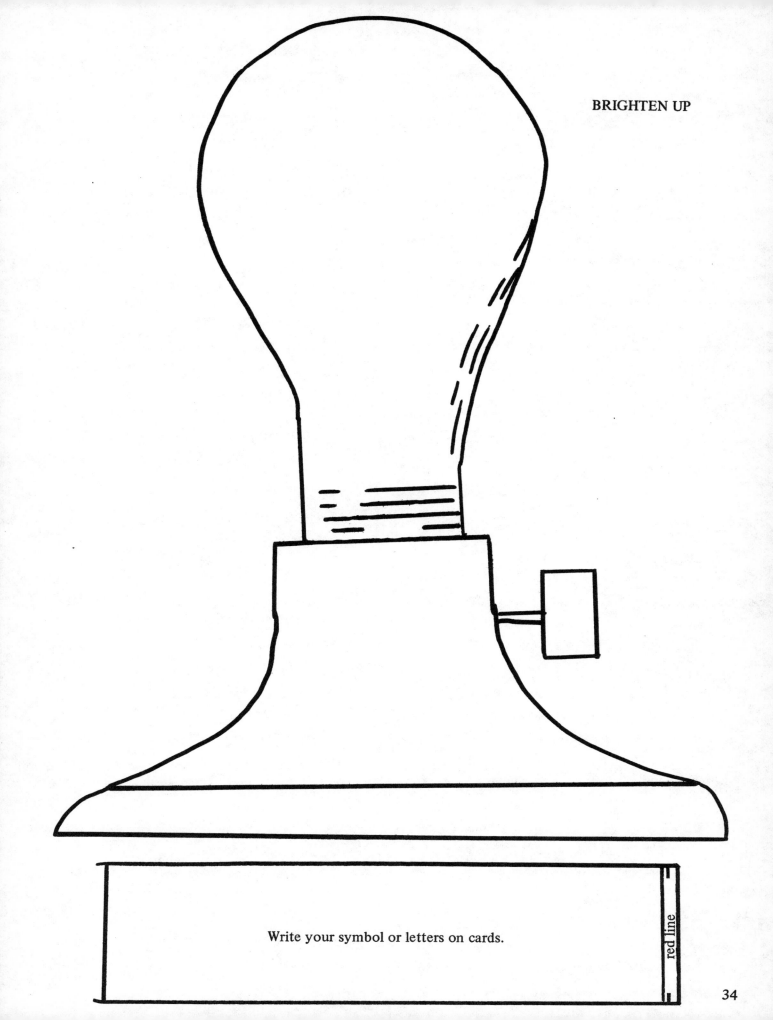

BRIGHTEN UP

Write your symbol or letters on cards.

red line

34

Name: Flower Family

Skill: Word families

Procedure: The child turns the center wheel to find new words. He learns the
                     initial sounds and ending sounds and which combinations make words.

Variations: Any word family group may be substituted.

Cut out the flower base and circle–attach the circle to the base with a brad.

FLOWER FAMILY

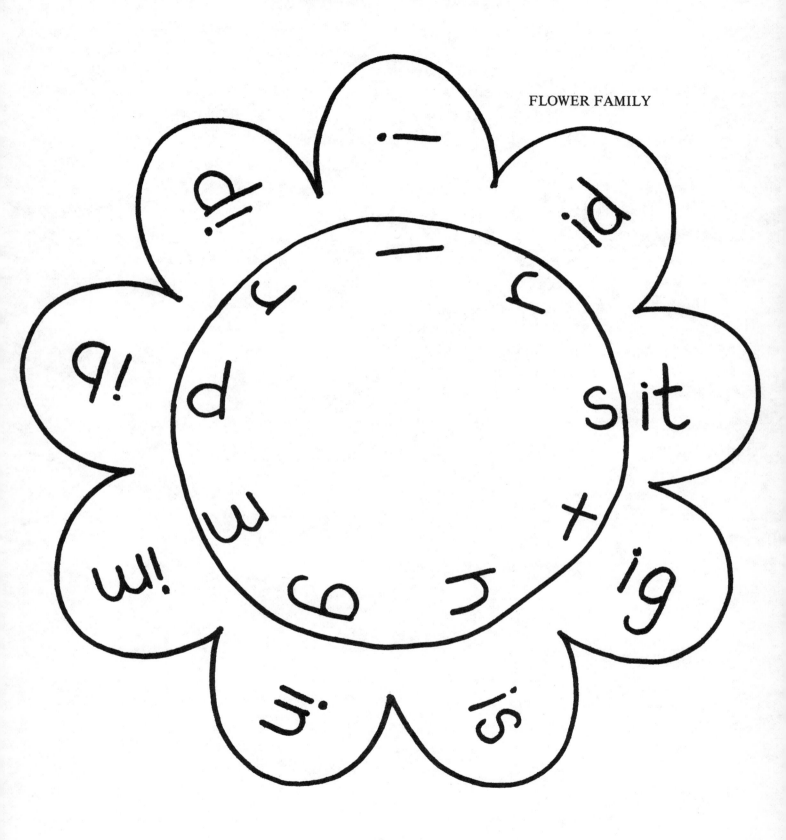

Name: Initial Sounds

Skill: Reinforcement of Initial Sounds A,B,C,D

Procedure: The child looks at the picture and decides what letter the
picture begins with. He then puts it in the envelope denoting
that sound. He can turn the card over for a self-correcting
activity.

Variations: Initial sounds and intial blends may be extended.

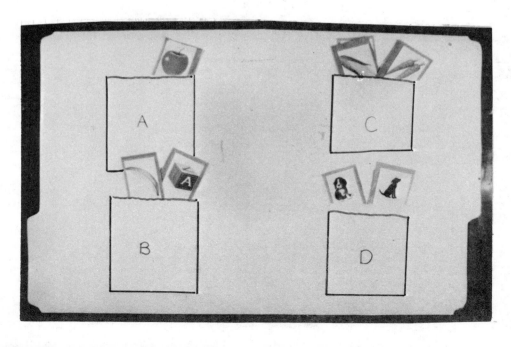

Glue your pictures or decals to cards.

INITIAL SOUNDS

Name: Rhyming Words

Skill: Matching Pictures and Words that Rhyme

Procedure: The child says a word by either looking at the printed word or picture then locates a word that rhymes with it. He can place the words in the envelopes. Symbols on the back of the cards make the game self-correcting.

Variations: The vocabulary can be extended to meet the child's level.

Glue your pictures or decals to cards.

Name: Classifying

Skill: Classification of Pictures

Procedure: The child looks at the picture card. He decides which
group noted on the envelopes that it goes with. He puts
the card into that envelope. Symbols or words on the
back correspond to the correct envelope to make the
game self correcting.

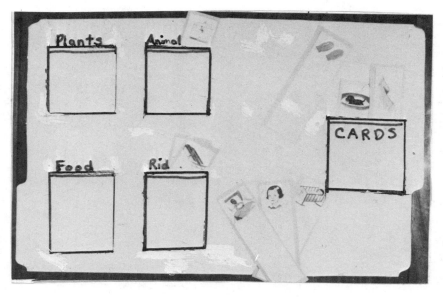

Glue your pictures or decals to cards.

Name: Weather/Community Helpers

Skill: Matching Symbols and/or Words

Procedure: The child places the words or symbols in front of himself. He looks at the symbol or picture on the folder. He then places the other word or symbol next to the picture that it matches. For example: the word *windy* matches the kite symbol and the fire truck symbol matches the fireman.

Variations: Any picture or group of pictures may be substituted. Words or symbols may be used for this matching exercise depending on the child's level and experience. Other common subject matter may include food and animal pictures.

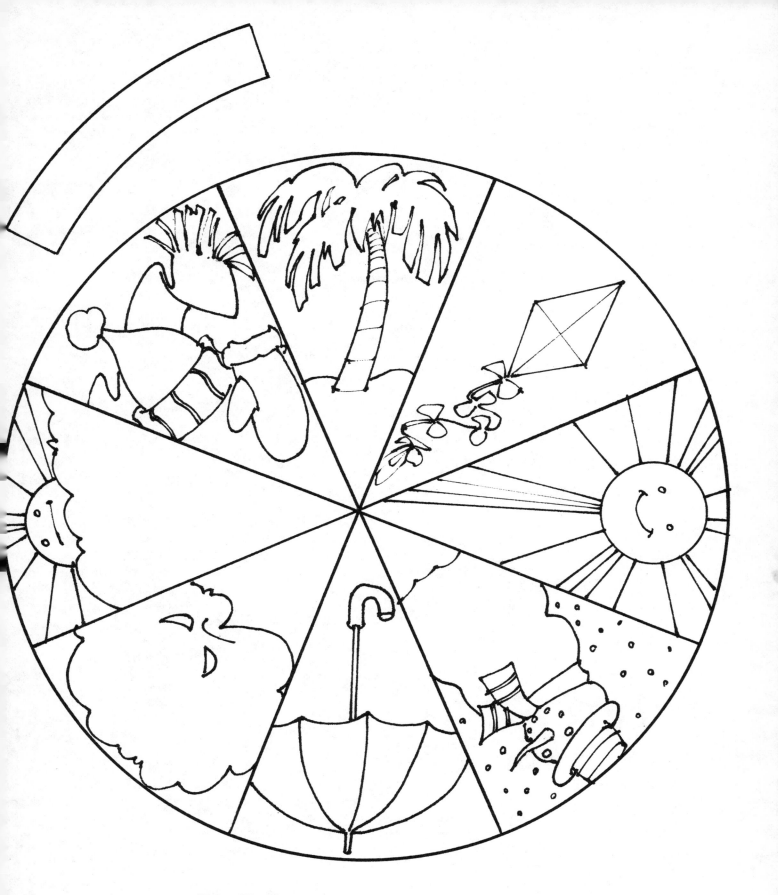

Title: The Weather

Instructions: Print the following words on strips of construction paper or tagboard: CLOUDY, WINDY, WARM, SNOWY, COLD, PARTLY CLOUDY, RAINY, SUNNY. Use these words to match appropriate weather symbol.

44

Title: Community Helpers

Instructions: Cut out the following four pictures and adhere
to manila folder.

Title: Community Helpers (con't)

Instructions: Cut out the following symbols and adhere to
tagboard. Use these symbols to match with
Pictures in folder.

US MAIL

part II
mathematics

Name: Seriation-Pencils, Rectangles

Skill: Seriation-putting objects in a series

Procedure: Pencils can be used to explain the seriation concept. The pencils are put in a series from short to tall or tall to short. Questions refering to the order may be asked.

Variations: Extend questions: Show me the tallest, first, last, etc.

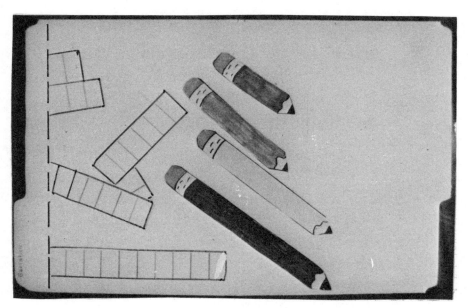

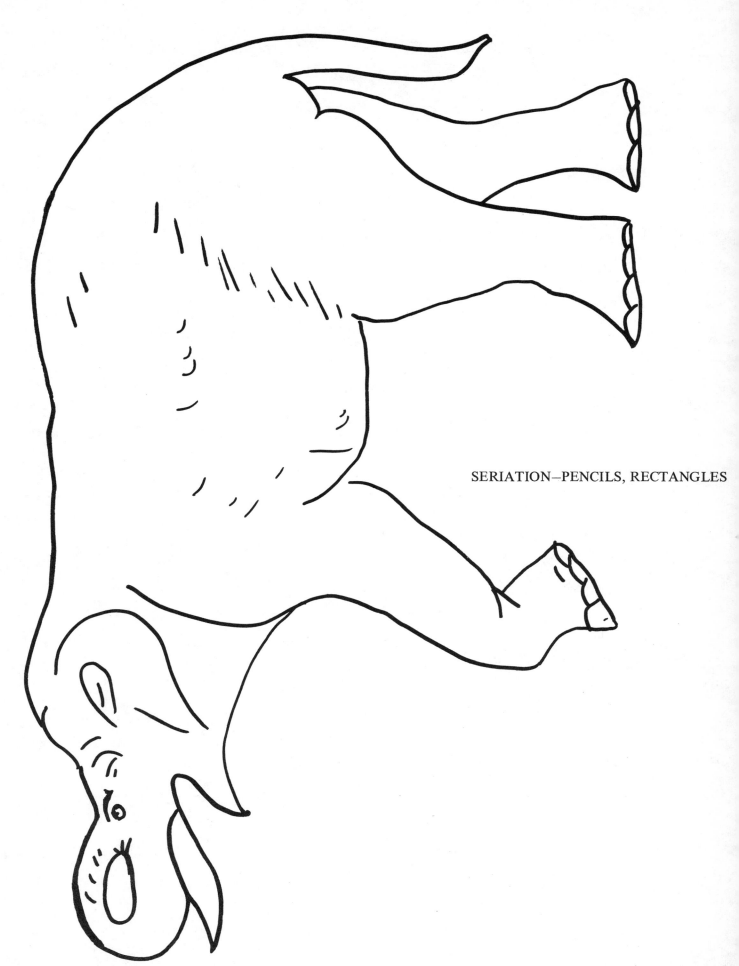

SERIATION—PENCILS, RECTANGLES

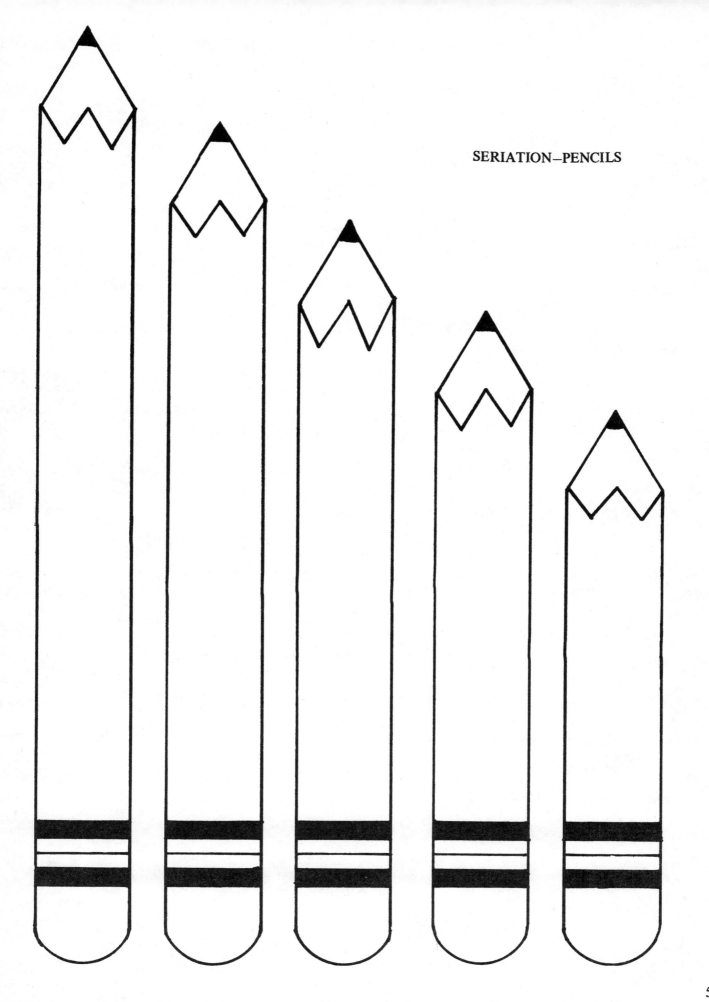

SERIATION—PENCILS

50

SERIATION—RECTANGLES

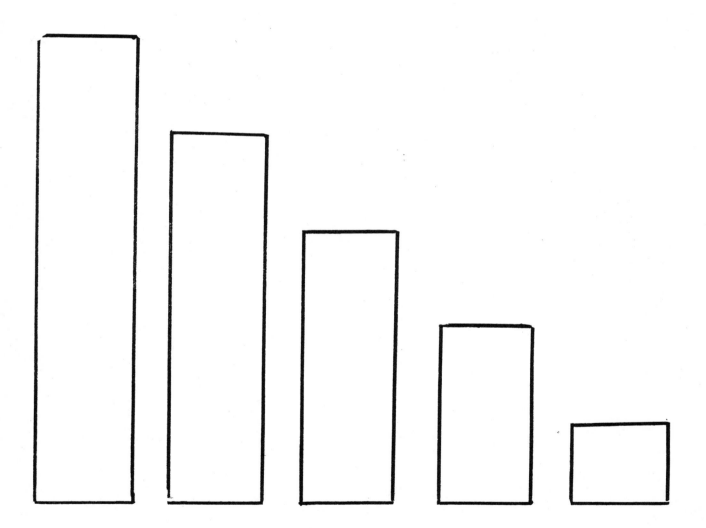

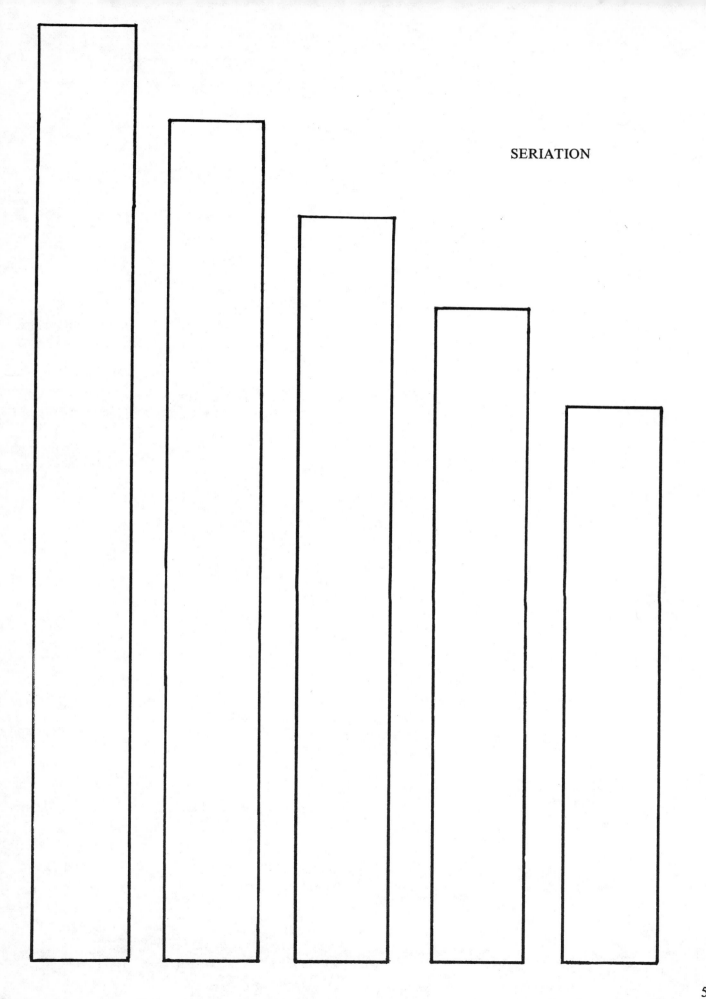

SERIATION

52

Name: Matching People

Skill: Matching Sets with Numerals 1-10

Procedure: The children with the numerals (or set of dots) are matched with corresponding number. The different children can be described to reinforce any objective such as cultural awareness, color, or dress.

Variations: The children can be used with different symbols, math combinations, or words (opposites).

Color the little people and then write the concepts you wish to teach on them.

Black hair
Brown Skin

Brown hair
White Skin

Black hair
Yellow Skin

Black hair
Brown Skin

54

Red hair
White skin

Black hair
Brown skin

Blond hair
White skin

55

Blonde hair
White skin

Black hair
Yellow skin

Brown hair
White skin

56

Name: Fishbowls/ Fish Dial

Skill: Number Sequence/ Math Facts-Addition or Subtraction

Procedure: The child can place the fishbowl in number sequence-the bowl
with one fish is first, two fish is second, etc. Verbal questions
may then be asked, such as "Show me the biggest fish" or "Show
me the last fish." The colors may also be noted. The answer dial
and the addend or minuend is attached to the fish. The child turns
the dial to see the problem. He can lift the gill of the fish to see the
correct answer.

Variations: The fishbowls can be extended and other verbal questions may
be asked. Any math fact may be used including multiplication
and division.

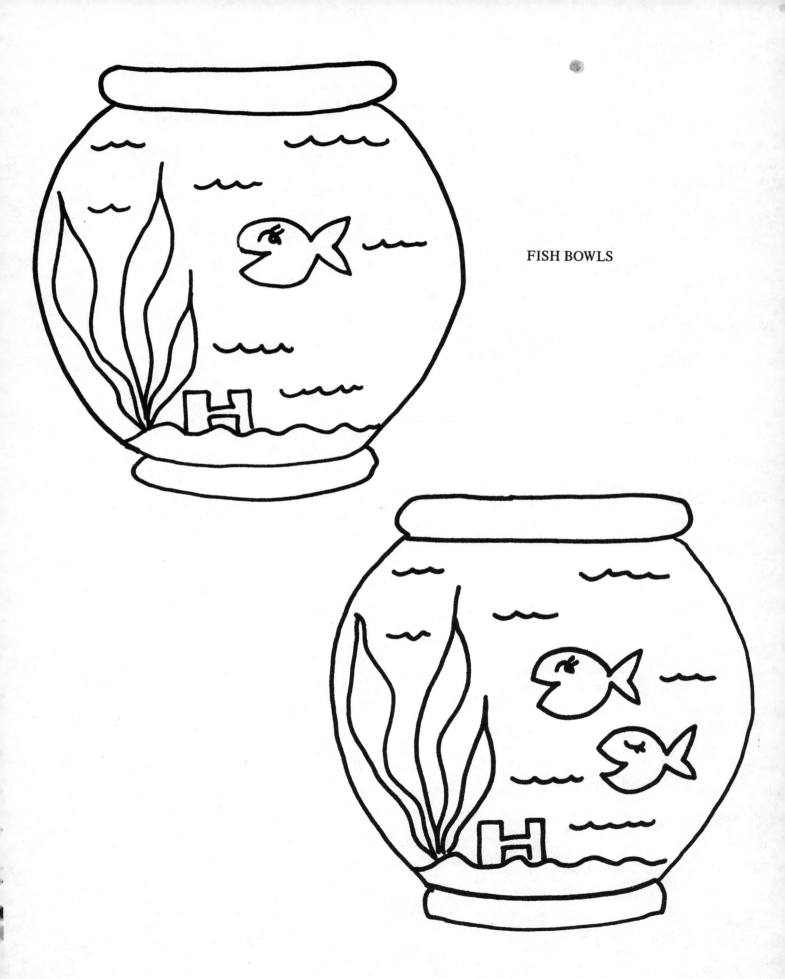

FISH BOWLS

58

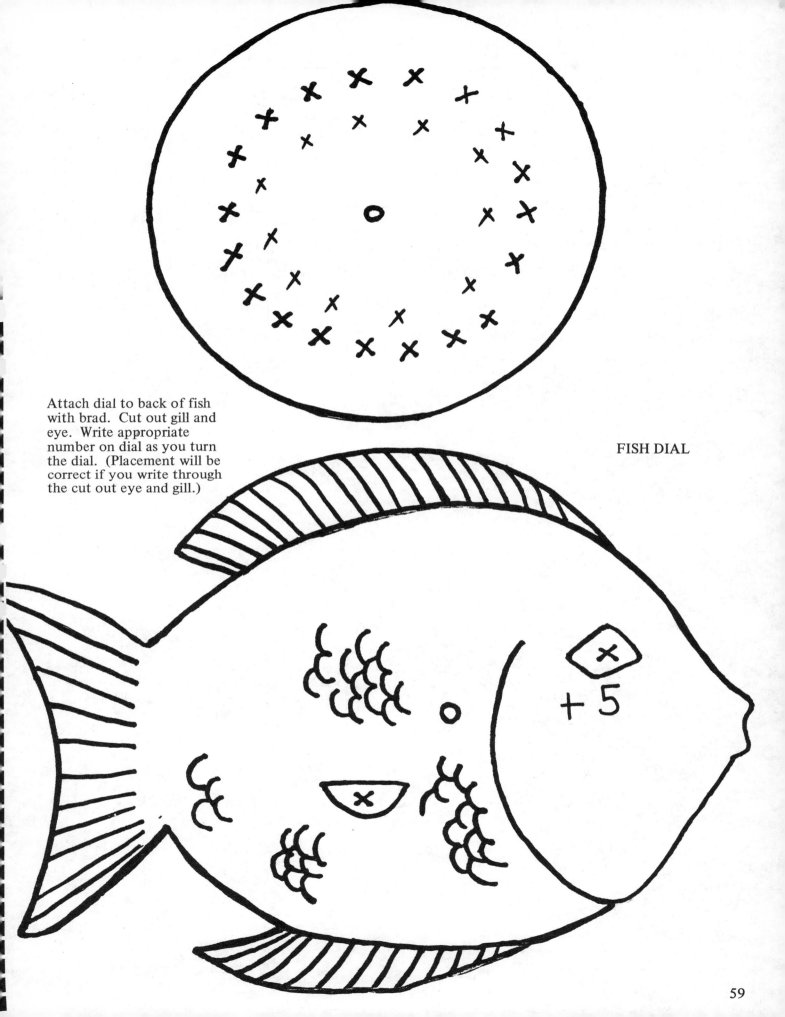

Attach dial to back of fish
with brad. Cut out gill and
eye. Write appropriate
number on dial as you turn
the dial. (Placement will be
correct if you write through
the cut out eye and gill.)

FISH DIAL

Name: Worm in the Apple

Skill: Math Facts

Procedure: The worm is placed in the apple. As it is slowly pulled out, a
math fact appears. The child answers the fact, then pulls the
worm a little more for the correct answer to appear.

Variations: Math facts, number word and numeral, upper and lower case
letters may be used on the worm.

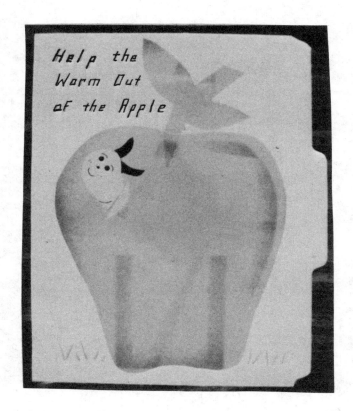

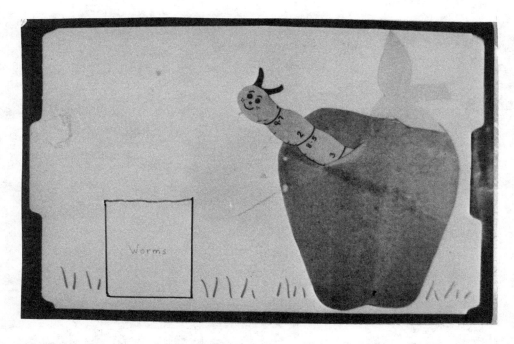

WORM IN THE APPLE

Cut here

$1+0$
1

$1+1$
2

$1+2$
3

$1+3$
4

$4-1$
0

$4-3$
1

$4-2$
2

$4-1$
3

Paste pattern onto tagboard. Cut out and color.

61

Name: Raindrops

Skills: Counting Numerals in Sequence

Procedure: The child places the raindrops on the board in numerical sequence. The correct placement of some numerals reinforces the correct placement. The child can count in sequence after he is finished to determine if he is correct.

Variations: The squares may be simplified or extended. The letters of the alphabet may be substituted for the numerals.

Small umbrella can be traced for outside of folder.

Cut out and trace left side of umbrella.
Flip over and trace right side.

Name: Tree Forest

Skills: Numeral Recognition and Counting; 1 to 1 Correspondence

Procedure: The child throws a die and moves the correct number of
spaces. He must say the number on the square to remain.
The procedure is continued until there is a winner. Other
skills such as sharing, social interaction and rules will emerge.

Variations: Any substition for the numerals may be made. For example:
letters, words, or math combinations.

TREE FOREST

Make gameboard with various trees and add concept to each square.

Name: Milkman

Skill: Counting to 10, Numeral and Set Construction

Procedure: The child reads the numeral on the door of the house, counts the corresponding number of milk bottles and places them in the slot. The numbers are in sequential order so number suquence is also reinforced.

Variations: Math combination could be substituted for the numeral and the child could count the milk bottles to obtain his answer.

Name: Ice Cream

Skill: Counting and Numeral Recognition

Procedure: The child reads a numeral on a cone card and places the correct number of scoops of ice cream on the cone.

Variations: Math combinations or number words could be substituted for the numerals for a higher level task.

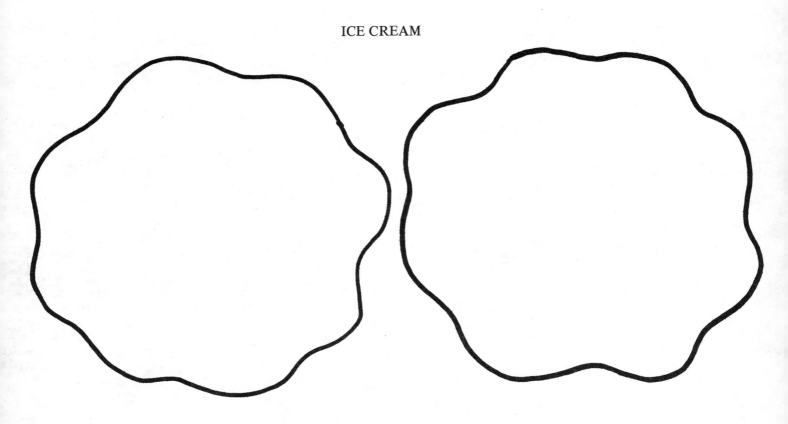

Cut out 10-Number from 1 to 10.

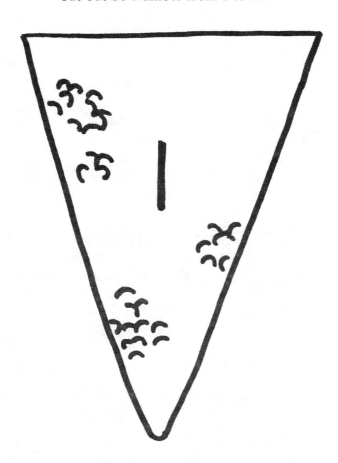

Name: Number-Set Cards

Skill: Counting Sets to 10: Number Word and Numeral Recognition

Procedure: The child counts the number of objects on the card and
matches the numeral-number word card. He can place the
cards in sequential order.

Variations: Other objectives may be emphasized as verbal questions are
asked. Vocabulary words that may be included are first,
fewer, more, less, most, least, and last.

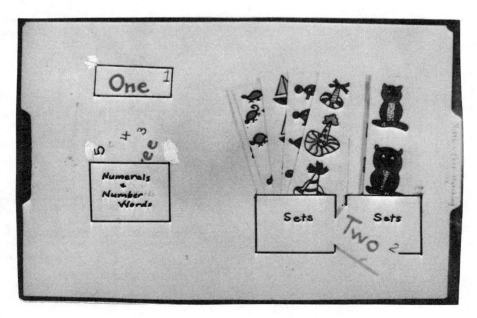

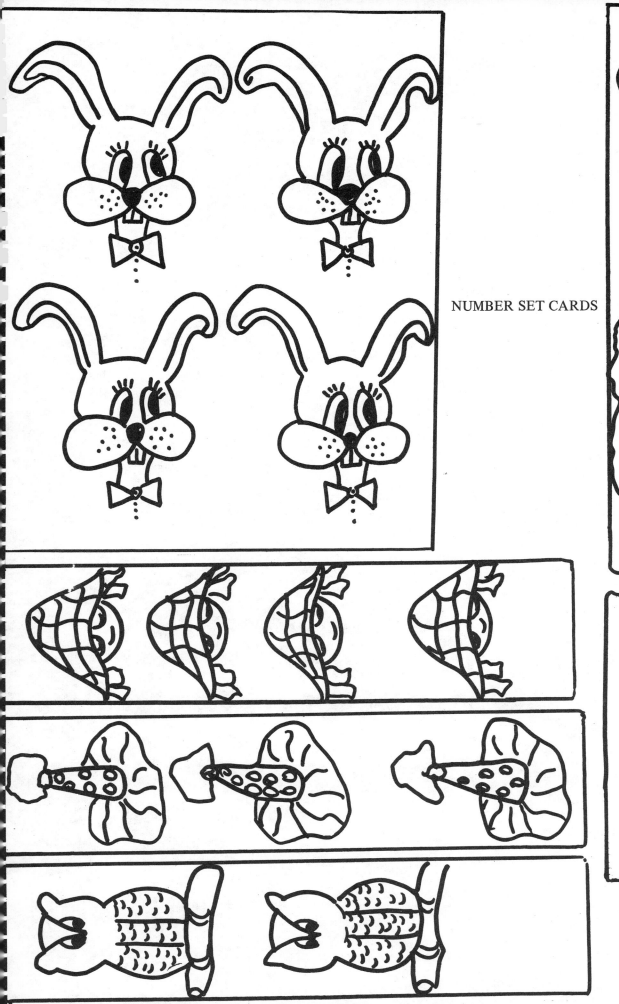

NUMBER SET CARDS

71

NUMBER SET CARDS

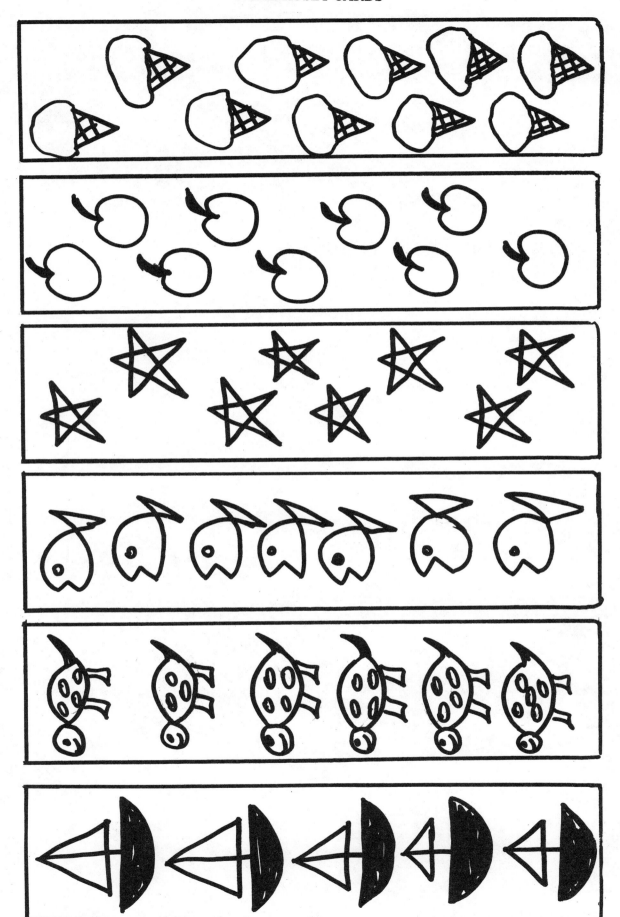

72

Name: Math Garage

Skill: Number Recognition, Counting to 10, Numeral-Set Matching

Procedure: The child counts the number of dots on the garage and then matches the corresponding numeral car. The cars and garage may be color coordinated for an easier task.

Variations: Math combinations with answers on the cars, numerals with number words on the cars, upper and lower case letters may be substituted.

To play the MATH GARAGE GAME trace and cut out cars numbered from 1-10 and garages dotted from 1-10 Each child is to match the number on the cars with the corresponding dots on the garage.

Name: Hatch a Match

Skill: Math Facts

Procedure: The child reads the math fact and locates the answer.
He puts the two pieces of the egg puzzle together and
if he is correct the puzzle fits.

Variations: Words may be written on the egg and the child can put
the word together.

HATCH A MATCH

Write combination on one side and answer on other side of
egg. Randomly cut down the middle.

76

Name: Money Match

Skill: Matching Coins

Procedure: The child matches the loose coins to the coins arranged
on the board. For more advanced task the coin combinations
can be emphasized.

Variations: Allow the child to count and learn values of the coins.

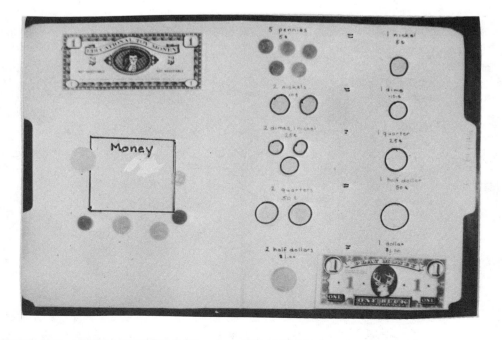

MONEY MATCH

78

Name: Fractions

Skill: Reinforcing the fractions 1/4, 1/2, 1/3 Utilizing the basic shapes

Procedure: The child combines the pieces of the shapes to form the whole shape. The fractions can be explained and noted as he is ready for the concept.

Variations: Smaller fractions can be made.

Cut into puzzle.

FRACTIONS

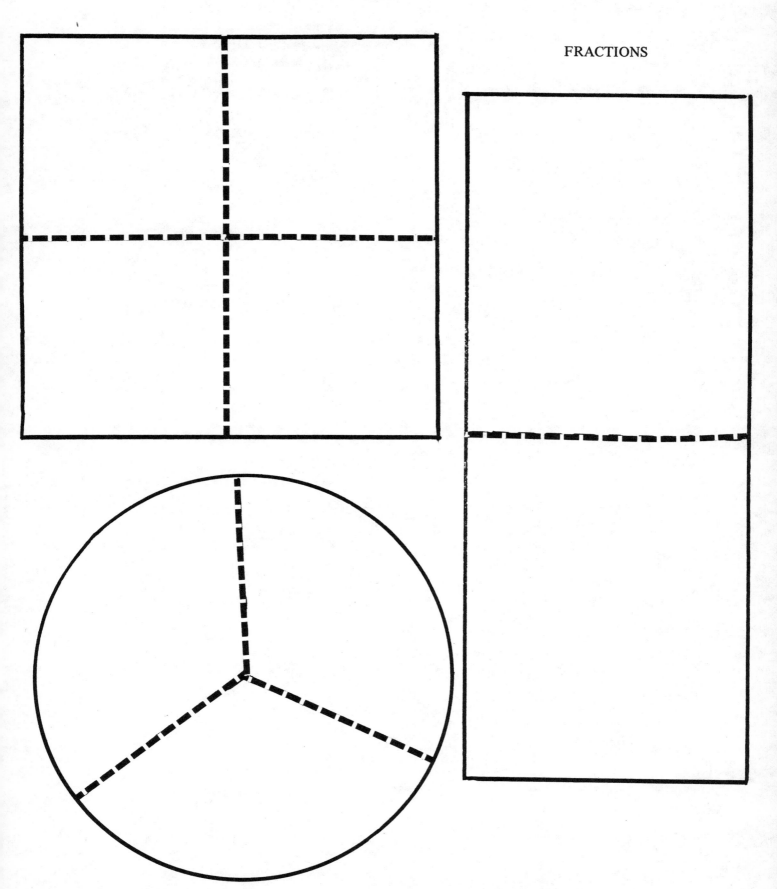

Name: Cars/Bird Houses

Skills: Math Facts Under 10

Procedure: The child places the license plates (or birds) in front of himself.
He says the combination then locates the answer on the car (or
birdhouse). He places the license (or bird) on the appropriate
space.

Variations: Any math combination may be substituted depending upon
the child's level.

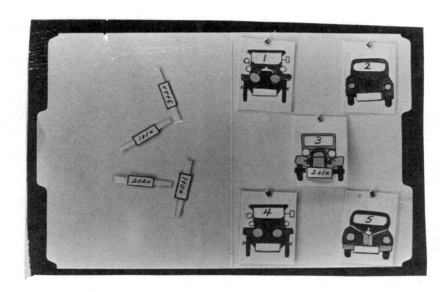

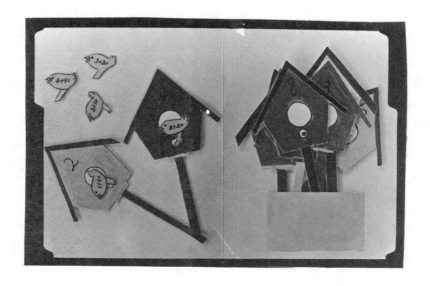

Write combination on license and answer on car.

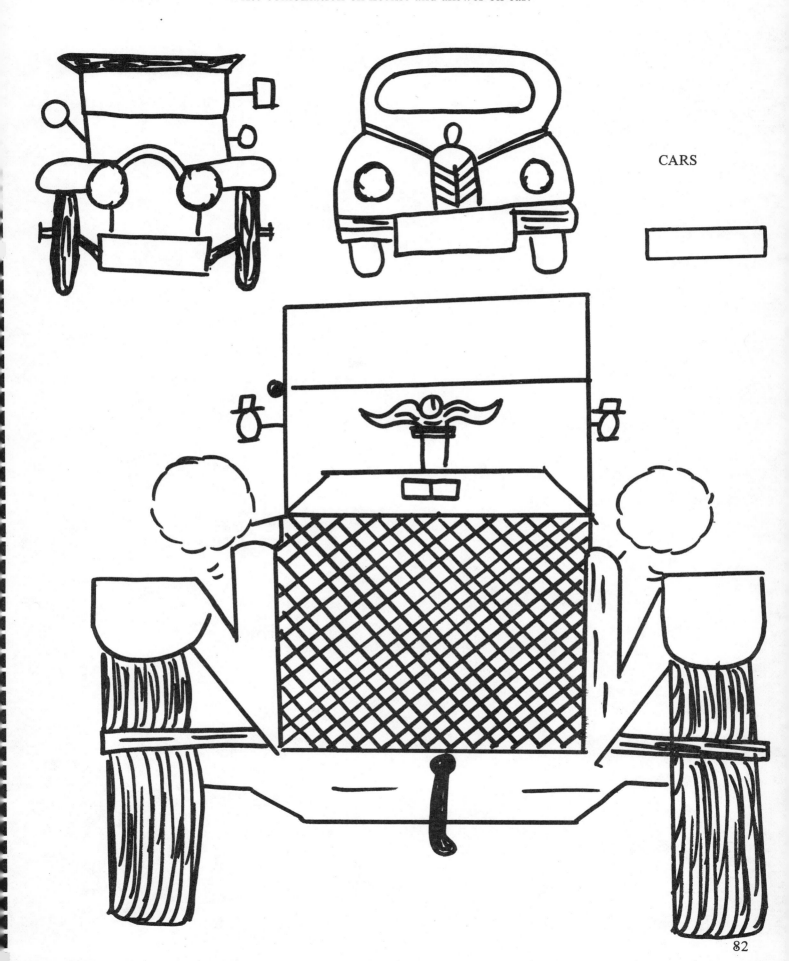

CARS

Write combination on bird and answer on house.

BIRD HOUSES

part III
general readiness

Name: Snake Puzzle

Skill: Color, Shape, Number Matching

Procedure: The child places the snake pieces on the board with the corresponding shape, color, and number.

Variations: Other symbols, letters, words, may be substituted for the numerals. The snake may be one color to omit the basic objective of color matching. The puzzle concept can be transferred to any drawing, such as the hound dog or giraffe.

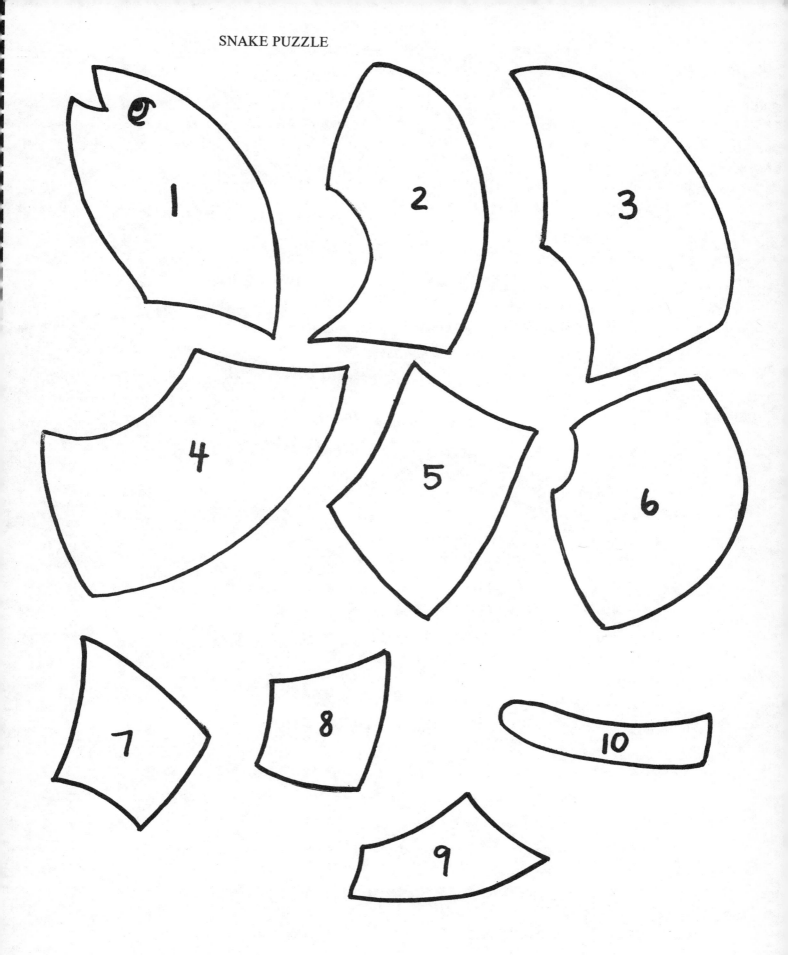

Name: Match a Mat

Skills: Visual Discrimination-Color and Patterned Wallpaper

Procedure: The child is shown how to match the two cards that look alike.
He then matches the set of mats with the mats on the board.

Variations: Paint samples, vinyl floor covering samples, sandpaper, minerals,
beans, shells, fabrics may be used depending on what is readily
available.

MATCH A MAT

Cut out two matching patterns.

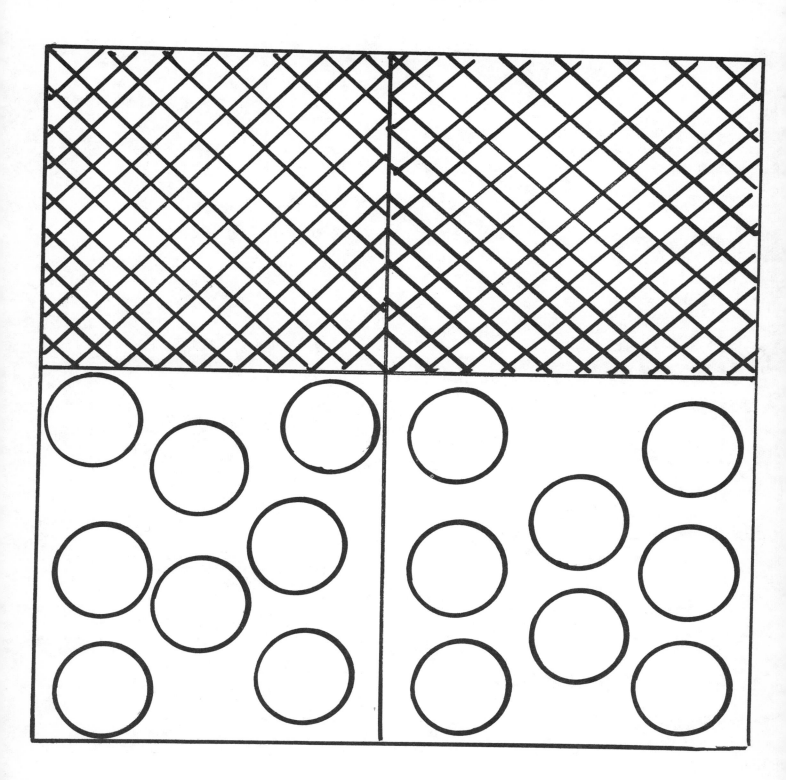

Name: Matching

Skill: Matching Symbols and Differentiating Between Alike and Different

Procedure: The symbol squares are placed on their corresponding symbol on the mat. The squares with the two objects are viewed by the child and he decides if they are alike or different. He then places them on the mat that denotes the correct spot.

Variations: Change the symbol to letter combinations or more complicated drawings.

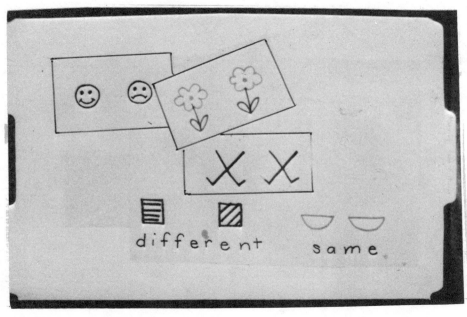

Sample card

MATCHING

Cut out 2 of each and match

Name: Matching Sequential Patterns

Skill: Matching Sequential Patterns

Procedure: The child can match the colored shape. Then he can place the same shapes under the noted pattern. Finally he can repeat the pattern. He can be asked to find certain shapes or colors.

Variations: Harder or easier patterns can be arranged.

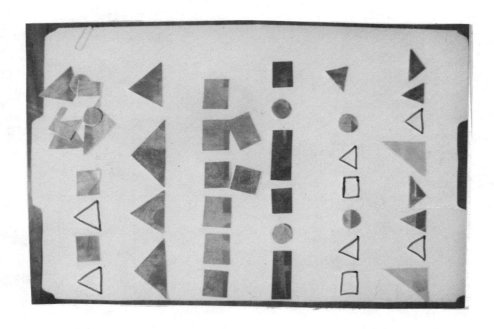

MATCHING SEQUENCIAL PATTERNS

Sample pattern.

Name: Draw a Shape

Skills: Recognition of Basic Shapes

Procedure: The child places the shapes into the pattern outlined on the
board. He can see shapes can make a picture. He may trace
around the cardboard shapes or on top of the laminated shapes.

Variations: Allow the child to draw his own pictures with basic shapes.

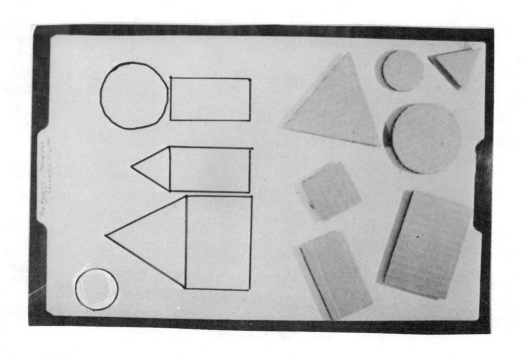

DRAW A SHAPE

Draw shapes on folder and make cardboard duplicates.

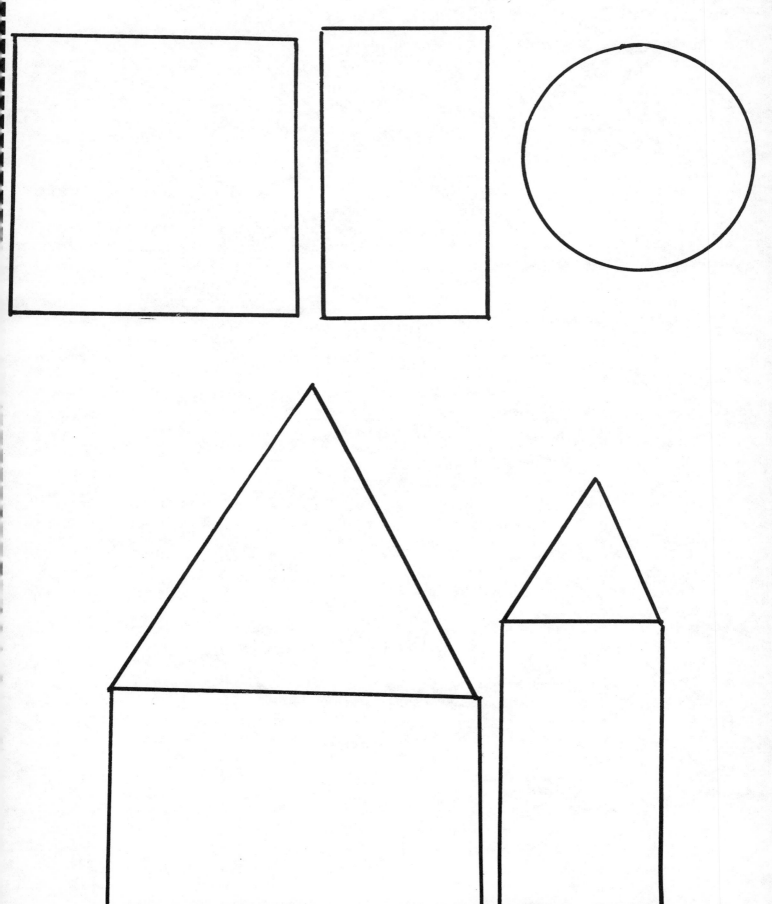

Name: Patterns

Skill: Color Recognition and Matching Patterns

Procedure: The child can put the colored square on top of the
corresponding square. He can then form the same
pattern on a blank card. The cards are in sequential
order from basic to more difficult.

Variations: Other patterns can be arranged by the child or teacher.

See snail pg. 15

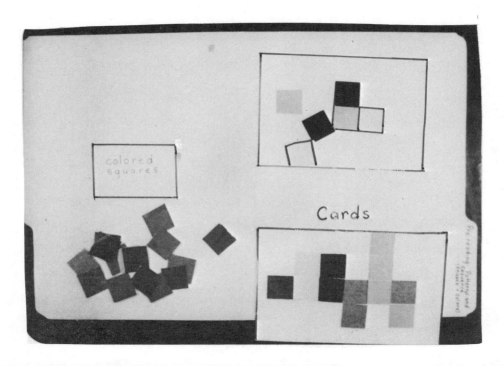

Name: Matching Faces

Skill: Matching Facial Expressions-Visual Discrimination

Procedure: The child looks at a face, finds the matching face on the
board and places his face beside it.

Variations: Other faces with more or less detail may be made. Verbal questions
regarding facial expressions may be asked.

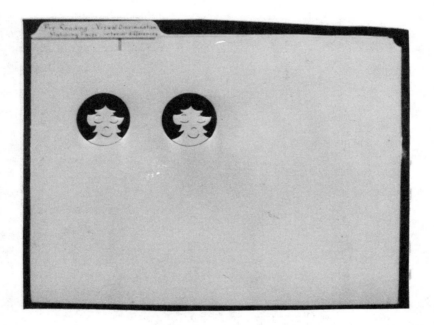

Cut out two sets of the following faces. Adhere one set to the manila folder as illustrated. Adhere the other set to tagboard and put in an envelope to use for matching faces in the folder.

Name: Screen Board

Skill: Visual and Tactile Symbol Recognition and Writing

Procedure: The child places a paper on top of the screen. He uses a crayon to make a letter or number. He then looks at and feels the symbol. The tactile experience reinforces the visual.

Variations: Any symbol may be written in this manner for reinforcement.

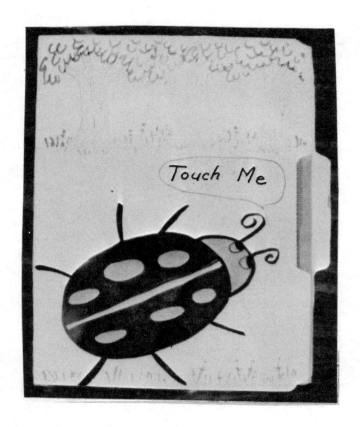

Name: Lacing Color Board

Skill: Word and Color Recognition-Fine Motor Development

Procedure: The child locates the color word and its corresponding
color. He then takes the yarn and places it in the hole
next to the color circle. (The yarn may have the corresponding color bead at the end for the basic level.) Figure
ground discrimination is also experienced as the child
crosses the yarn.

Variations: Any objective may be accomplished with this basic format.
Examples are upper and lower case letters, antonyms, math
combinations, and words with pictures.

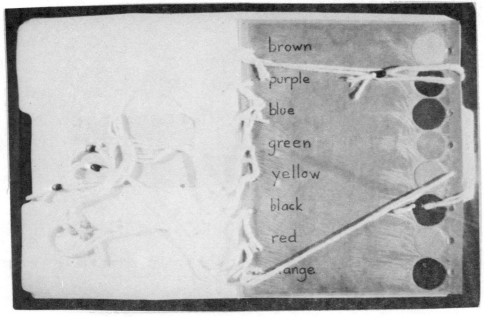

Name: Dressing Kit

Skill: Fine Muscle Development Using Zippers, Buttons, Lacing

Procedure: The child is instructed on how to zip, button, and lace. He
then uses the examples for practice and reinforcement.

Variations: Snaps, hooks and eyes, and other fine muscle fastening devices
may be added.

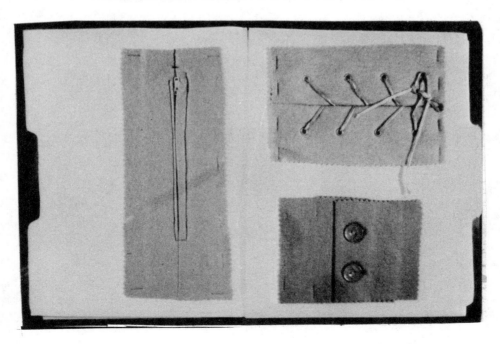

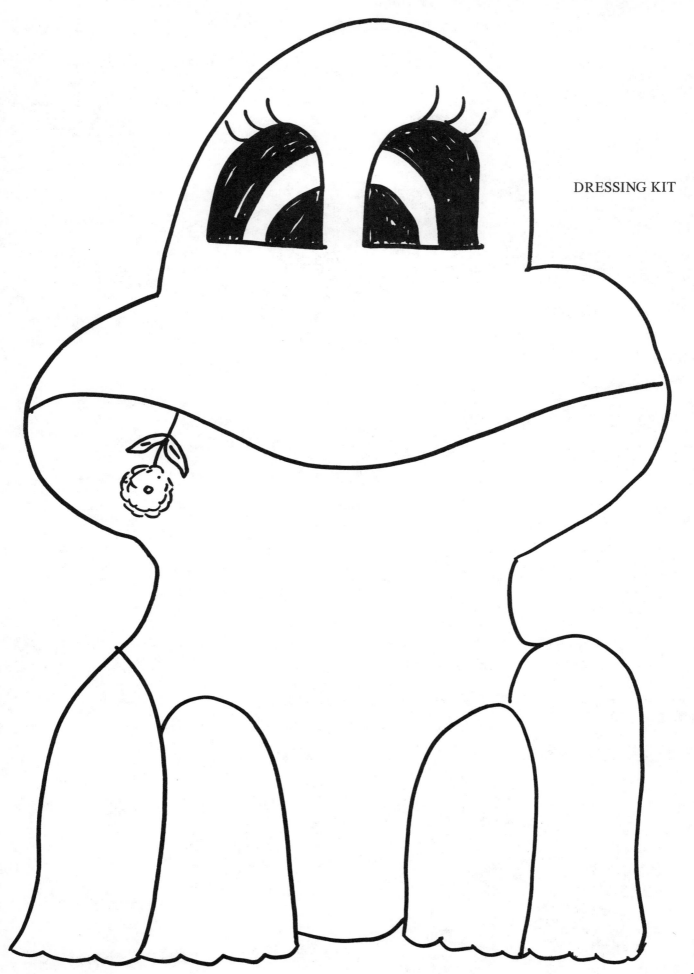

DRESSING KIT

Name: Classifying Shapes

Skill: Classification

Procedure: The child is asked to put the shapes in groups. His level of
of classification is noted by his ability to classify by color,
size, shape, and dots. (One half of the shapes have a black dot
dot in the center.) There are 64 shapes:

4 large green circles	4 large green squares	4 small green squares	4 small green circles
4 large yellow circles	4 large yellow squares	4 small yellow squares	4 small yellow circles
4 large red circles	4 large red squares	4 small red squares	4 small red circles
4 large blue circles	4 large blue squares	4 small blue squares	4 small blue circles

Variations: Ask the child to classify by a second method.

CLASSIFYING SHAPES

Name : Match a Puzzle

Skill: Visual Discrimination

Procedure: Two pieces of an identical drawing are used. One is mounted and
the other is cut into pieces. The child places the pieces over
the identical pattern.

Variations: Use simple or complicated patterns depending on your objectives
for the child. Wallpaper, magazine pictures, pictures of the
children may be used.

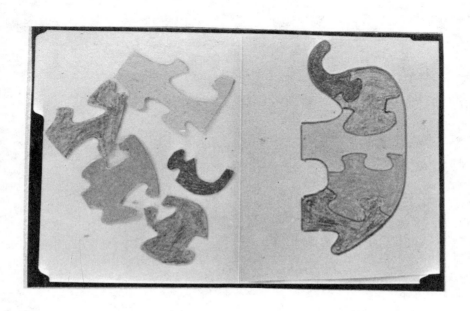

Color and cut out.

Name: Shapes

Skill: Matchi ng Colored Shapes and Combining Shapes to Make a New Shape

Procedure: The child can use the colored shapes to match the shapes on the board. He may use the shapes noted at the top of the card to make the new shape on the bottom of the card.

Variations: Designs may range in difficulty according to the child's level.

With these 3 shapes, make the large picture.

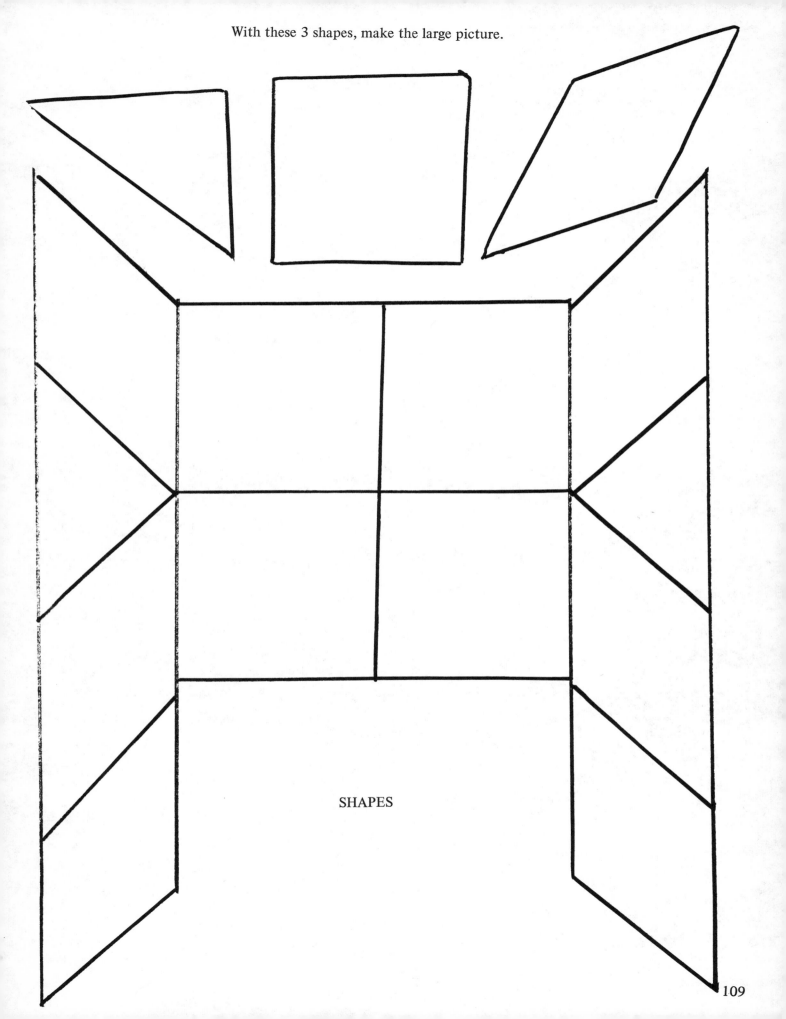

SHAPES

These are only a few examples of games and activities which you can make to provide a more enjoyable and productive classroom.

These activities are designed for particular children; therefore, it's up to *you* to make *your* activties NOW for *your* children.

MY COMPLETED FOLDERS

Name:

Number:

Date Completed:

Problems/Comments:

Some of the folder games in this book are reprinted from
The Handbook of Learning Activities for Young Children
by Jane Caballero, Humanics, Limited, 1980.